AF228429

The rat is red.

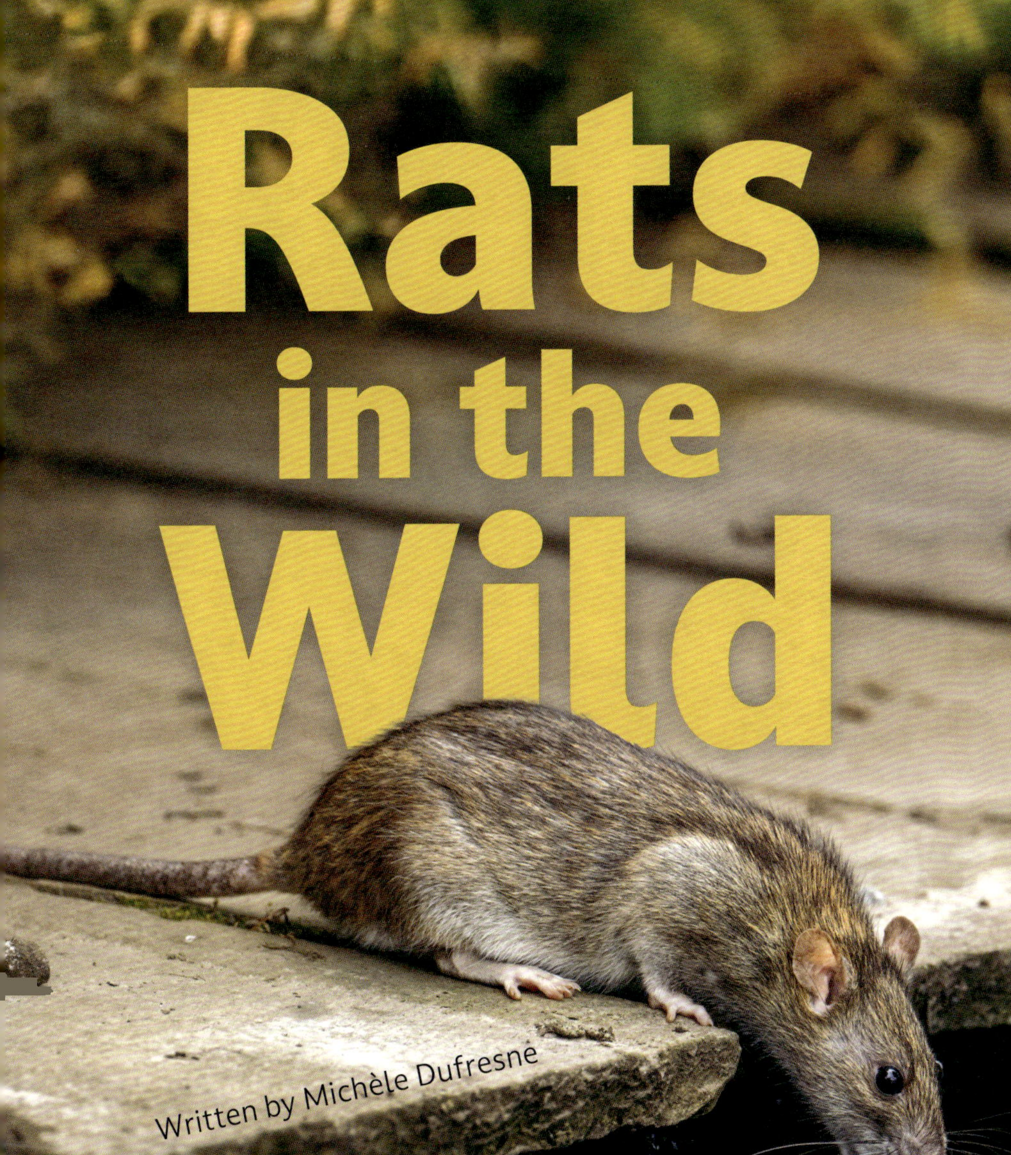

Rats in the Wild

Written by Michèle Dufresne

PIONEER VALLEY EDUCATIONAL PRESS, INC.

A rat can run.

Wild rats are fast runners and can travel up to several miles in a single night to find food!

Rats dig and **rub**.

Rats use their paws and teeth to dig and explore. They often rub against walls or objects to leave scent trails.

The rat hid in a **rug**.

Rats like to hide in soft, dark places to stay safe from predators.

A rat got rid of a bug.
Rats will sometimes eat bugs as part of their diet. They are omnivores and eat many different things.

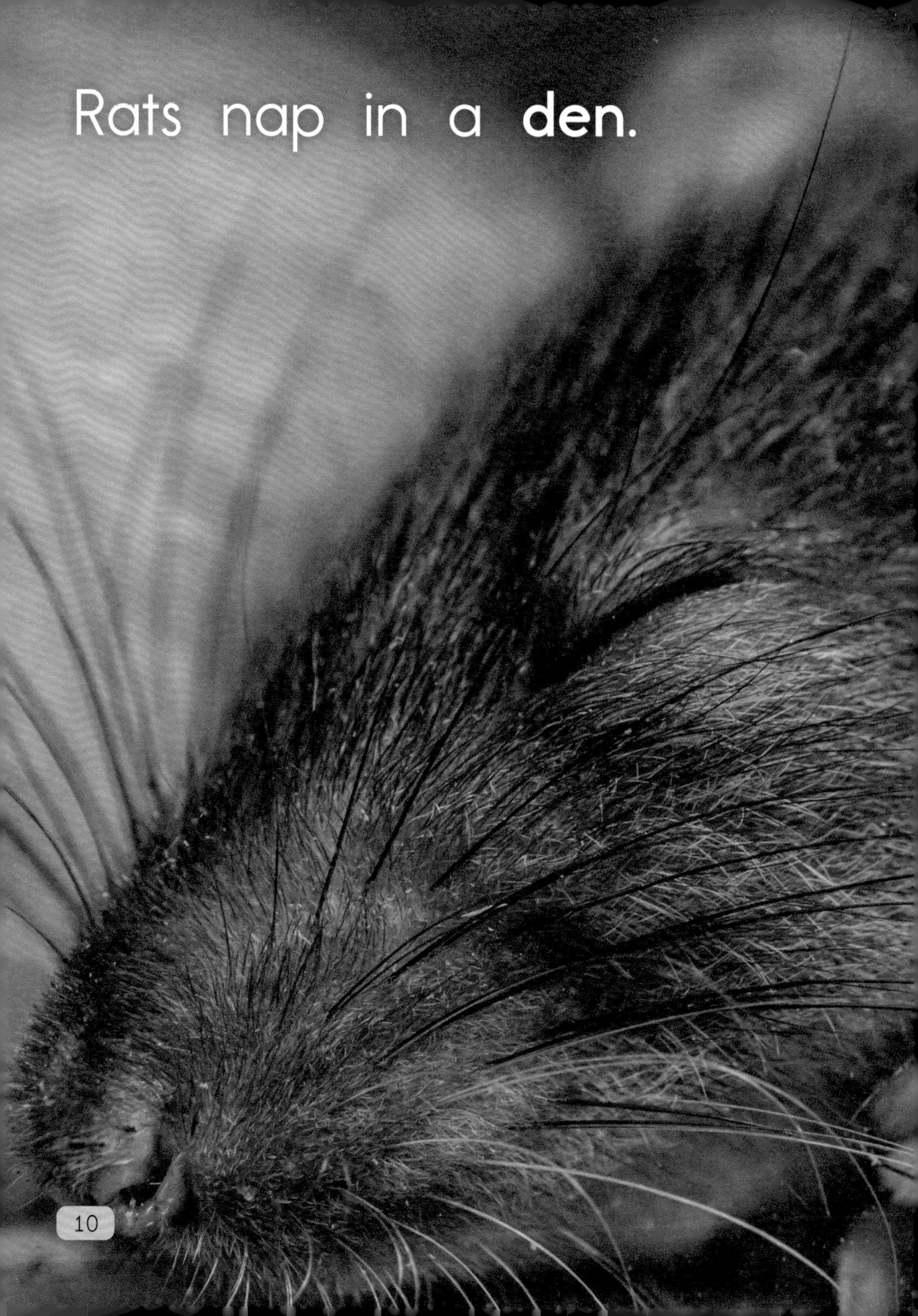

Rats nap in a **den**.

Wild rats build nests or
dens in hidden spots.
They use leaves, paper,
and cloth to make a
cozy sleeping space.

glossary

rub

rug

den